COACH'S
Little Book of Wisdom

Hints, Tips, and Insights
for Coaching Kids

Other Books in the Series:

Teacher's Little Book of Wisdom
Babysitter's Little Book of Wisdom

Little Book of Wisdom Series

COACH'S
Little Book of Wisdom

Hints, Tips, and Insights
for Coaching Kids

by Ron Quinn

GUILFORD, CONNECTICUT

Text design by Claire Zoghb

Library of Congress Cataloging-in-Publication Data is available.

ISBN 0-7627-2688-1
Manufactured in the United States of America
First Edition/First Printing

To all of the coaches who have modeled, molded, and guided my coaching beliefs and practices.
And to my good friend and mentor, Dr. Tom Fleck.

CONTENTS

Introduction 1

The Player 5

Coaching Wisdom 19

    Before You Begin 19

    Practice 26

    Game Time 41

    Sportsmanship and Competition 48

    Thoughts on Coaching 53

First Aid: The Injured Player 73

Wisdom for Players' Parents 81

About the Author 87

INTRODUCTION

Coaching is an art and a science as well as a profession. In fact, there are probably more people involved in coaching than in any other profession. People become youth coaches for many reasons: a love of the game and of competition, a desire to work with children, a coaching shortage in the community. Whatever your reason for becoming a coach, there is no doubt about it: Coaching can be a time-consuming, exhausting commitment. It is also one of the most rewarding things you can do for yourself and for your community.

This book is not intended to be a coaching manual, but rather a source of helpful insights, information, and humor. I hope it will help you through difficult times, provide a philosophical foundation for your endeavors, and make it easier for you to identify what is truly important when it comes to coaching children. The thought-provoking comments have been written to help you create a healthy, growth-enhancing, and rewarding experience for your players—whether you win or lose. In years to come, maybe someone will remember you as an individual who played an influential role in his or her life.

Even though it is a coach's job to teach, guide, and inspire others, sometimes coaches need a little instruction and advice, too. It has been reported that fewer than 20 percent of those who are coaching youth sports have received any training in *how* to coach. I have stated on numerous occasions, while conducting coaching education programs around the country, that coaching and playing are two different things. *Playing* sports doesn't necessarily prepare you to *coach* sports. And coaching children is a completely separate endeavor. So I strongly encourage you to pursue some type of coaching education program in your particular sport.

With heavy competition and poor sportsmanship dominating youth sports at times, it is wise to take a step back and be reminded that no matter how high the stakes may seem, these are children and it is only a game. Introducing children to the world of competition, physical activity, and good sportsmanship can be a valuable, life-altering experience for you and for the children who look up to you. So put on your sneakers, sweatshirt, and whistle, and remember: Children at Play, Proceed with Care!

THE PLAYER

Children at Play: Proceed with Care.

For children, joy is just being part of the game.

For young children, effort equals ability.

Child-centered coaching *is* coaching.

Children will perform and learn best in an environment with a lot of positive reinforcement.

Decisions should be made to develop each player. The team will take care of itself.

Children participate in sports to learn new skills, seek out new challenges, and to be with friends. A coach should make these his top priorities.

Children participate in sports to have fun!

All of your players deserve your attention and your respect, regardless of their level of ability.

Always treat every player on your team, regardless of age, gender, or ethnicity, with the same respect, kindness, and level of encouragement.

When you are explaining to players under age six what the various lines on the soccer field mean, don't bother asking, "Which line am I standing on?" The answer will *always* be "The white line!"

Players under age seven only know one playing direction—the direction the ball happens to be going.

Don't worry about getting your players psyched up to play; they are already wound up. Your job is to calm them down.

"The pick and roll cannot be taught to eight- and nine-year-old basketball players."
—*Bob Bigelow, former Boston Celtic*

In T-ball, players will never field the ball. They'll just chase it down until it stops rolling.

There is a difference between coaching men and coaching women. Coaching children is a completely different matter. They are not little men and little women.

The decision-making process can be learned and reinforced within youth sports.

Players should be provided with ample opportunity to make their own decisions.

Physical activity should not be used as punishment. Children should enjoy moving and exercising.

"There are no elite athletes under the age of twelve, only the least worst player."
—*Bob Bigelow, former Boston Celtic*

Avoid comparing children.

Children have trouble catching balls not because they are uncoordinated, but because their visual tracking skills are not fully developed until around age twelve.

Because young children have difficulty determining the direction and speed of a ball, they will miss and drop more than they catch.

Children age six and younger have a high center of gravity. They are top-heavy and can fall easily when they change direction. They also *like* to fall.

Gross motor skills develop before fine motor skills.

Give children only one task at a time. Anything more will short-circuit them.

How do you keep your players from bunching up? You don't!

Children six and younger don't understand the concept of a "team." A four-on-four-game often becomes seven-on-one.

At age ten, team identification becomes important.

Very young children have no sense of pace—it's go all out or take a bathroom break.

"Play is the key to open many doors."
—*Dr. Marianne Torbert, Temple University*

At around age twelve, boys and girls begin to develop differently and they prefer to play on separate teams.

Never label a player you can give a name to. "Clumsy" or "Shorty" is not a name.

Make sure a player's nickname is welcomed.

Don't talk to your players about their parents unless you have something wonderful to say.

Learn the difference between independent and antisocial behavior.

Accept your players for who they are, not who you expect them to be.

There are more success stories about late bloomers than young superstars.

Babe Ruth hit 714 home runs. He also struck out more than 1,300 times.

Late bloomers need encouragement—
how else can they bloom?

Never laugh at a player's answer
(unless it was supposed to be funny).

If you create a discipline plan *with*
your players, they'll be more apt to
follow it.

Building trust with your players
takes time, effort, understanding,
and consistency.

Children would rather play on a losing team than sit on the bench of a winning team.

Given the opportunity, players will often find the position that suits them best.

The hardest thing about teaching young children how to swim is how to put their suits back on.

Children are easily distracted. Don't take it personally if you are upstaged by a butterfly on the field.

By the age of eight, players should be able to carry their own equipment.

Players should be allowed to solve their own problems while their coach facilitates the process.

COACHING WISDOM

BEFORE YOU BEGIN

Questions you should ask yourself:

- Why do I want to be a youth coach?
- Why do we have youth sports?
- What are my responsibilities to each player, to the team, to the community, and to myself?
- What will I enjoy most about coaching children?
- What will I do to improve my coaching?

Coaches should clearly define
their objectives and principles before
they begin.

Your coaching philosophy should include
statements about your beliefs, motivation,
methods, and experiences.

It is the coach's responsibility to
provide proper instruction, equipment,
and supervision.

It is the coach's responsibility to make a
fair and impartial selection of players.

Unfortunately, "late bloomers" are being cut from youth teams in favor of the bigger, faster, stronger—but not necessarily better—player. Children under the age of twelve need time to develop.

Cutting a child from a team can be devastating to the child.

Don't cut children from teams. Create more teams—and put more kids on the path to better personal performance.

Success requires players and a good coach.

Leave your coaching or playing credentials at home. Players under the age of ten will not be impressed.

Your first assignment after the team has been formed is to establish the drink and snack list.

Allow the players to choose the team name—it's *their* team.

Be sure that all your players
understand the basic rules and concepts
of the game, but realize that they may
not remember them *during* the game.

Create a mission statement for your team
and be sure to include both parents and
players in the process.

It is imperative that you create an
atmosphere that is safe, secure,
and appropriate both physically
and emotionally.

Youth sports are designed to be simple.
Don't complicate them.

Make sure all players are wearing shoes
that fit *today*, not shoes they will grow
into tomorrow.

Conduct a preseason meeting with
parents to discuss practice and game
schedules, emergency procedures, and
team goals.

Appoint a team Mom or Dad to help
with team management.

Be open to suggestions and participation from parents.

Goals are meant to be set, attained, and revised.

Always have plans B, C, and D ready.

PRACTICE

Coach with consistency. You set the tone and standard of playing behavior.

During practice, you have less than thirty seconds to get an activity moving before your players move on their own.

A youth coach trains and prepares his team partly through appropriate activities and instruction and partly by just letting them play!

Instruction should be given in a clear, concise, and correct manner—your players don't need a dissertation.

Do not play games or conduct activities of elimination. Who wants to sit out and watch the "good" players?

In soccer, if you ask your players to put the ball in the back of the net, be prepared to watch them throw it over the goal.

Never ask your players for a ball. You will get them all at once. Ask a particular player for his or her ball.

Practices that are highly organized and efficient are not necessarily effective.

The learning process does not follow a predictable pattern. Allow for some chaos.

Initiate developmentally appropriate activities—exercises and games that meet the physical, mental, and social needs of children within a particular age group.

Coaches should progress from simple to complex activities as players reach certain levels of skill and understanding.

All activities and exercises should have implications for the game. If they don't, change them.

Focus on achieving team and personal goals rather than only on winning.

Achieve success by setting and attaining realistic goals.

Season goals should provide opportunities for children to improve their interpersonal and leadership skills.

You can only teach children accountability by giving them responsibility.

You can only teach children responsibility by holding them accountable.

Rewards should be unexpected.

Keep practices FUN!

Every child should have an equal
opportunity to be successful.

Always try to increase the number of
turns and the chances for success.

Don't spend too much practice time
on repetitious drilling. Drills are
static and boring.

Activities and games should be fun,
dynamic, and encourage creativity.

Activities and games should
allow freedom of movement and
decision making.

Present activities that have a sense
of adventure.

No player should be permanently
eliminated during a practice session.

If the practice activity involves some
form of elimination, make it temporary.
Have the player perform a task to get
back in the game.

Activity Checklist:

- Does this activity have an objective?
- Are ALL players involved in the activity?
- Are creativity and decision making being used in this activity?
- Is the space being used appropriate for this activity?
- Is your feedback appropriate?
- Do the activities have implications for the game?

Blocked practice—repeating the same movement over and over in exactly the same way—should be used in sports in which the environment is predictable: archery, swimming, bowling, baseball, and when executing football plays.

Random practice—performing a task or skill in a variety of ways, changing distance, speed, or direction of the task each time the skill is performed—should be used in sports in which the environment is unpredictable: soccer, basketball, tennis, and ice hockey.

Certain aspects in some sports may require a combination of blocked and random practice, such as restarts or specific plays.

Coach your players to discover the game for themselves. They shouldn't expect you to teach them every aspect of the sport.

Allow your players to introduce and teach a game.

Give a player time to share a story or experience before practice.

Keep a journal of activities that work and your players enjoy.

If an activity catches your team's interest, there is nothing wrong with repeating it frequently.

When asking your players why an exercise is not working, give them the time to solve the problem.

Teach your players that their feet will always get their hands to the ball.

"The Zone" of effective coaching is somewhere between overcoaching and undercoaching.

Overcoaching is when you are more tired than your players after a game or practice. Undercoaching is when you didn't even break a sweat.

Overcoaching is when your players look at you for every move. Undercoaching is when your players can't find you.

Overcoaching is when your players wait for you to give them permission to play. Undercoaching is when your players show up thirty minutes before practice to get a game in.

Overcoaching is when your players never get a chance to ask a question. Undercoaching is when your players never ask a question.

In soccer, teach your players to move to where the ball will be, not to where the ball is.

In tennis, the person who hits the most balls in wins the point.

When in doubt, lob.

At the first sign of lightning, call the game or practice off and take your players off the field!

Instead of *telling* a player to do something, *ask* him or her to do it.

Consequences are not punishments. Using consequences in practice will increase focus and competition.

Doing five quick push-ups would be a consequence. Fifty push-ups would be a punishment.

When a player under the age of eight wants to go to the bathroom, give the entire team a bathroom break. They'll all need to go anyway.

GAME TIME

To reduce any confusion during the game, always determine your substitution order *before* the game.

A great way to determine who will play and when is to create a chart. Assign each player a number and rotate the necessary amount of players, in order of their number, per quarter (inning, period, etc.). If you continue this throughout the season, each player will have equal playing time.

Resign yourself to the fact that spectators will never understand every nuance of the sport.

Remember that the field situation is always changing. Be sure to keep that fact in mind when you are giving instructions from the sideline.

Don't get your daily workout running up and down the sideline during a game. You will find the game much more enjoyable from a sitting (or standing) position.

At halftime, don't discuss what your players *didn't* do; chances are they already know. Tell them what they *need* to do in the second half to be successful.

Halftime speeches shouldn't be long-winded: Your players won't remember them.

During halftime, let your players get water, talk to each other, and stretch. Let them know who will start and give them a few suggestions just before the next half begins.

Postgame talks should be kept to a minimum. If they lost, they won't want to hear it. If they won, they won't think they need it.

The best time for a postgame discussion is at the beginning of the next practice.

When an individual or team plays well, tell them.

When an individual or team doesn't play well, don't tell them. They already know.

When discussing a loss or a poor performance, focus on specific aspects of the play, not on the players.

When giving constructive criticism, use the "psychological sandwich." Begin with something positive, followed by the necessary information, and finish with something encouraging.

Allow your players to develop their own pregame warm-up routine.

When playing in a tournament, never look past your current opponent.

Tournaments should be organized for the players, not for the number of games or the money to be made.

When every T-shirt you own has a tournament logo on it, you know you've been to too many.

Make sure parents know how to make
an effective tunnel for players to run
through after a game.

A plate of cookies or brownies will
take the sting out of the most
disappointing loss.

SPORTSMANSHIP AND COMPETITION

Young players play with a great deal
of fairness and sportsmanship, but
when they feel pressured by adults to
win, they will often sacrifice good
sportsmanship to do so.

Fairness and sportsmanship are the
most important qualities to be cultivated
in any player.

As competition increases, good
sportsmanship decreases.

Playing the game for fun is far more important than winning it.

If you can't stand losing, you shouldn't play the game.

Competitiveness burns from within.

Do not allow players to reprimand other players.

Competition is an opportunity to be challenged and to grow; it's not a war against an enemy.

Meaningful competition comes out of good sportsmanship.

Do not tolerate poor sportsmanship.

Encourage strategizing; forbid cheating.

Poor sportsmanship can come from anyone, even from your best player.

A high level of stress within a competitive environment can turn a child away from the enjoyment of physical activity.

Unfortunately, the term "lost childhood" is often associated with organized youth sports.

One of your goals as a coach should be stress prevention.

Do not measure success by games won or lost.

When playing in games with your team, let them win often.

Attribute success to ability and effort.

Teach your players to give and
receive praise.

THOUGHTS ON COACHING

Coach's Motto: Be Patient, Be Positive, Be Flexible, and Have Alternatives.

Once you accept a coaching position, you have a legal duty and a moral obligation to look out for the health and welfare of your players.

Give praise generously.

Effective coaching is avoiding the three Ls: Lines, Laps, and Lectures.

Happiness is seeing a player you
coached years ago and hearing him
call you "Coach."

The Coach of the Year should be the
coach whose players all return the
following year.

Encourage your players to organize
their own pickup games, whether it's
soccer, baseball, volleyball, or basketball.
This allows them to learn about the
sport outside of practice.

Teach your players to be confident in
their decisions.

Let your players know you may not
always be able to solve their problems.

Coaching is both an art and a science.

If you are coaching children, being a
parent or a former athlete is not enough.
You must seek an accredited coaching
education program.

A coach can have as much influence on a
child as a teacher or a parent.

As the coach, players look to you for guidance. Be sure that what you are telling them is correct.

Feedback is information about a skill or movement just performed. It can be general ("That was a great throw!") or specific ("Swing your leg in the direction you want the ball to go.").

Positive feedback states what was done correctly.

Negative feedback details what was not done or what was performed incorrectly.

The positives should *always* outweigh the negatives.

Paralysis by analysis occurs when too much feedback prevents players from learning to rely on their own skills and decisions.

How to prevent Paralysis by Analysis: Don't make a habit of constantly telling players what to do and how to do it. Let them try to figure things out on their own.

Problem-solving skills can only be developed if you give your players problems to solve.

In addition to youth sports, neighborhood games still play an important role in child development.

Playground and neighborhood games allow children to resolve differences, create strategies, and adhere to their own rules. Try to apply this to your coaching.

Coaches must make an effort to teach
children problem-solving, leadership,
and critical-thinking skills as much as
they teach them how to hit a baseball
or throw a football.

We have to make a concerted effort to
keep youth sports a kid activity.
Otherwise it becomes a formal activity
organized by adults for children.

The Roman philosopher Cicero
emphasized the importance of childhood
activities in the first six years of a child's
life to his overall lifetime development.

Plato (427–347 B.C.) stated that children between the ages of three and six should be absorbed with play and games that they create.

French philosopher Jean Jacques Rousseau (1712–1778) believed that curiosity and play should be used to promote learning.

German educator Friedrich Froebel (1782–1852) fostered the idea that learning can happen during play and games.

Child psychologist Jean Piaget (1896–1980) believed that children perceive the world differently than adults.

Psychologist Bruno Bettelheim (1903–1990) supported and promoted the idea that play allows children to be "in control." This contributes to the development of a sense of security and self-sufficiency.

Child psychologist and educator Erik Erikson (1902–1994) viewed play as a vehicle that allows children to attempt to deal with and overcome problems.

Erik Erikson also considered play as a way for children to learn to organize life and integrate various experiences.

The TIONS of Effective Coaching:

- Preparation
- Organization
- Explanation
- Demonstration
- Participation/Execution
- Correction
- Evaluation
- Reflection
    —*Dr. Dave Carr, Ohio University*

Don't be afraid to make mistakes (just be sure to learn from them).

Encourage your players to ask questions.

Know when *you* need to ask questions.

Be a good listener.

Be a *better* observer of practice and playing behavior.

Yelling prevents you from observing and analyzing the game.

Let your players know you
enjoy coaching.

It's OK for your players to know a little
more than you do.

Value the work done by the ground
crew, parents, and assistant coaches.

Coach by example.

Look to improve something about your
coaching every day. It can be as simple as
making a few more positive comments or
introducing a new activity.

Encourage your young players to attend a high school or a college game.

Encourage your players to read about their sport.

Teach your players that punctuality is important.

Remember that children under the age of sixteen are not driving themselves to practice.

The coach should always be the last person to leave after a practice or game.

Always be sure that your players leave with the appropriate person following a game or practice.

In coaching, you should always work for quality rather than quantity.

As a coach, you may find talking to yourself will limit questions from parents. However, you'll find that you talk to yourself anyway.

As long as you enjoy coaching, your players will enjoy playing. The moment that you *don't* enjoy coaching, your players will sense it.

Keep your players so active during practice that they'll sleep well at night.

Yelling at your players is still *yelling*, regardless of your intent.

There is a big difference between yelling and calling out instructions.

Games should be modified to meet the needs of your athletes.

Coaching is a profession whether or not you are paid.

Coaching should be a passion whether or not you are paid.

Life is serious, sport is a game—so lighten up and have fun.

For some people sport is serious; try your best to reeducate this group.

Coach the child, not the game.

Good coaching is encouraging
your players to drink Gatorade after a
hard game.

Great coaching is having Gatorade
dumped on you.

Success is 10 percent physical and
90 percent mental. Unfortunately,
as coaches, we often focus 90 percent
on the physical and only 10 percent
on the mental.

Things that coaches say, but shouldn't:

- If you're tired, don't show me.
- You're getting beat like a drum.
- When in doubt, kick it out.
- Just run it off.
- Your brother/sister never played like that.
- You can do this—it's easy.
- If you're not going to give me the effort I want, why did you bother to show up?

Your role as coach is to provide practice activities and exercises that give every player a chance to succeed.

Your role as coach is to present practice activities and exercises that create the maximum number of opportunities to perform the task.

Your role as coach is to present practice activities and exercises that encourage players with different ability levels to work with each other.

You are a role model. Take that
role seriously.

The experiences gained and
lessons learned in youth sports will
last a lifetime.

Coach so that when a child says "Coach"
it is said with a smile.

When all else fails: ICE CREAM!

FIRST AID: THE INJURED PLAYER

Injuries in youth sports are increasing.

Whenever a player is injured, all players should freeze and sit down. Comments like, "Wow, you're bleeding!" are usually not well received by the injured player.

For children, all injuries are serious— just ask them. If a child believes he is hurt, then to a certain degree, he is. Treat the injury emotionally as well as physically.

"Know your personal skills and abilities when it comes to injury assessment and treatment."
—*Dr. Brett Massie, Xavier University*

Your emergency action plan should be more than "Call 911!"

Always remain calm—you're the coach!

When a player is injured, inform a parent or guardian immediately.

After an injury has occurred, follow up on your player's condition as soon as possible.

A *sprain* is an injury to the ligaments that attach bone to bone. Treat with ice.

A *strain* is an injury to the muscles and tendons. Treat with ice.

When in doubt, put ice on it.

For most muscle, joint, and soft-tissue injuries, use the RICE method: Rest, Ice, Compression, and Elevation.

Never tell an athlete to "run it off."

Never complicate an injury.

Never underestimate an injury.

Children are prone to heat-related illness.

Heat cramps are largely due to dehydration and usually occur in the calves or abdomen.

Signs of heat exhaustion:

- Cold and clammy skin
- Below normal or elevated temperature
- Profuse sweating
- Nausea

To treat heat exhaustion: Make the child rest, drink lots of cool fluids, and get out of direct sunlight.

Signs of heat stroke:

- Hot, dry skin
- Red and then gray skin
- An elevated temperature

To treat heat stroke: Cool the child's body by removing clothing and packing ice around the head and under the armpits.

If you believe a child is suffering from heat stroke, get the child to a medical facility *immediately*. Heat stroke that goes untreated can lead to serious illness or death.

Learn cardiopulmonary resuscitation
(CPR).

Remember to check the ABC's: Airway,
Breathing, and Circulation.

Do not move an unconscious child.

Never use ammonia or smelling salts on
an unconscious child.

Know emergency phone numbers
in advance.

Always have first-aid equipment accessible and in good working order.

When in doubt, always err on the side of caution.

"Sometimes the decision not to play a player based upon the severity of the injury is an integral part of the player's recovery."
—*Dr. Brett Massie, Xavier University*

A medical doctor should determine when a player is ready to return to practice.

WISDOM FOR PLAYERS' PARENTS

If you can't take your child getting knocked down in a game, perhaps he or she is still too young.

When your child comes off the field or court after a game, your first question should be "Did you have fun?" not "Did you win?"

Excessive yelling and cheering only confuses the players and coaches; try to keep it to a minimum.

According to the National Center for Educational Statistics, less than one percent of all children playing organized sports will qualify for a college athletic scholarship.

If you are paying for camps, clinics, tournaments, lessons, and trainers because you expect your child to win a college scholarship, you are better off putting your money in the bank.

Participation in youth sports should be an end in itself, not a means for future stardom.

Predictions about the future potential of an athlete under the age of thirteen are accurate less than 25 percent of the time.

Do not risk your child's enjoyment of the game by creating unrealistic goals that he or she is unlikely to attain.

Parents have tried to place their children in organized sports as young as three years old! Is prenatal sport far behind?

Most preschool children are not ready for team sports.

Children do not need to specialize in a particular sport until their adolescent years. Early specialization can result in early burnout.

Things that parents say to children,
but shouldn't:

- You really disappointed me.
- You should have won that game.
- I'm spending all this money and I expect a better result.
- I can't believe that you missed that shot.

Champions are products of sacrifice, but youth sports should be the pursuit of excellence through competition and appropriate child development.

ABOUT THE AUTHOR

O ne of the leading experts on youth coaching, Dr. Ronald Quinn has been coaching for nearly thirty years and has earned national recognition for his participation in the world of youth sports. For the past ten years, he has been the Head Coach of the women's soccer team at Xavier University in Ohio, where he has earned more than one hundred career wins. Dr. Quinn is also Associate Professor and Director of Health, Physical Education, and Sport Studies at Xavier, a member of the United States Soccer Federation's National Teaching Staff, a major contributor to the development of the National Youth Coaching License, and serves on the U.S. Youth Soccer Coaching Committee. In 2000, he was honored as Ohio Coach of the Year by his fellow coaches. He lives in Cincinnati, Ohio, with his wife and three sons.